Thresholds
Poems

Books by Douglas W Anderson
Libros por Douglas W Anderson

A Promise — Poems
Una Promesa — Poemas

In the Light of the Sun — A Witness Poems
A la Luz del Sol — Un Testigo
Poemas

Eurydice Turning — Poems
Euridice Volteándose — Poemas

Realization Into the Changing Light Poems
Realización En la Luz Cambiante
Poemas

Thresholds
POEMS

Douglas W Anderson

"It is quite true what philosophy says: that life must be understood backwards. But then one forgets the other principle: that it must be lived—forwards."

–Søren Kierkegaard

"It was not of the gods, but of Men themselves!"
After Aeschylus - The Persians

–Douglas W Anderson

Copyright © *Thresholds* 2020 by Douglas W Anderson and Quaking Aspen Press

All rights reserved. No part of this book may be used or reproduced in any manner whatsoever without written permission except in the case of brief quotations embodied in critical articles and reviews.

Published 2020 by Quaking Aspen Press www.quakingaspenpress.com
Printed by KDP/Amazon Co on demand.
Author Page on Amazon, Douglas W Anderson

Thresholds: Poetry / English

Excerpt from *The Light of the Stars: Alien Worlds and the Fate of the Earth* by Adam Frank. Copyright 2018. WW Norton & Company, New York, page 219. Used by permission.

Excerpt from *The Diary of Søren Kierkegaard* Ed. by Peter Rhode. Copyright 1993. Carol Publishing Group Edition, New York, Page 111. Used with the kind permission from The Philosophical Library and Editors, Philosophical Library Inc., editors@philosophicallibrary.com

Excerpt from *The Seven Plays in English Verse-Aeschylus* by Lewis Campbell. Copyright 2013. HardPress Publishing, Miami Fl, Page 85, Line 392. In the public domain.

Excerpt from *Ancient Greek Philosophers* by Canterbury Classics. Ed. April Farr, et al. Introduction by Ken Mondschein, PhD. Copyright 2018. Canterbury Classics - Printers Row Publishing Group, San Diego, California. Page 341-342. In the public domain.

Cover Photograph by: Ralf Roletschek,
www.flickr.com/photos/roletschek/albums, www.roletschek.at
Used by permission.

Book Cover Design and Book Layout by: Lieve Maas,
Bright Light Graphics, www.brightlightgraphics.com

Back cover Photograph by: Pamela A Anderson

Printed in the United States of America

ISBN 978-1-733622-639
LCCN 201991459

In Memory Of

Merrick Robert Pierce LCPL USMC
Died Thua Thien S. Vietnam 27OCT67
On The Wall Panel 28E Line 85
Willamette National Cemetery
S - 2487

ACKNOWLEDGMENTS

The men I have coffee with at the "store" or the "coffee shop" have contributed to this volume unseen. Ed, Bob, Dennis, Walt, Robert, Chuck, Keith, Chuck, Darrell, Jack, Steve, Warren, Herm, Dean, and so many others who come in and out seasonally. We do not speak about politics or religion, only philosophical history, great thinkers, complex mathematical theorem's, electricity, magnetism, chemical engineering, electrical engineering, rocket science, communications systems, space and gravitational waves. Sometimes we get off track on to Jungian psychology applications and archetypes. Not often enough though.

Lieve Maas of Bright Light Graphics in Bend Oregon, is a graphic artist who puts things, including this book, together. She is invaluable in all aspects of publication and advice.

The photograph on the front cover by Ralf Roletschek is unique and reveals the beautiful arch thresholds in the Upper Lusatian Library of Sciences, Görlitz, Germany. One has to pass through these thresholds where open sources of knowledge can advance important questions. Ralf learned English in school in East Germany until free in 1982.

The individuals who have been involved in reading various poems, their helpful comments, criticisms, and editing were all important in their interpretations. I sometimes didn't see some of what they saw. They helped me answer the question "What have I done for the reader?" Thank you in so many respects.

DEDICATION

The first poem in this book emerged from a childhood memory. It started as an awareness. Since it has been a lurking presence in my thoughts. I believe everyone at times has an isolated epiphany or two that becomes important as they go through the experience of life. I sensed there was something else out there in the world I wanted to be part of but did not understand what it was. It was the beginning of my spiritual journey, such as it was, at eight years old.

I remember one night in particular. It had been snowing for days. The weather was cold for weeks in Portland. The 39th hill was closed for sledding. We had a grand time in those days from morning till late at night. The snow reflected the brightness of the street lights so we were able to see at night like it was day.

It was a time of peaceful bliss for a kid. Although there were wars that occurred somewhere in the world, we were not very aware of them in our youth. The radio carried most of the news. Some kids did have a transistor radio. My parents purchased a black and white television set. We could not watch it often. Prior to that we would go over to my grandmother's house, watch a program and go home to bed. They lived across from where I grew up on 38th street. A wonderful place to grow up when the snow would stay for weeks.

When the snow melted it would go away fast with those warm Chinook Winds, as they used to be called. We would go back to school resuming where we left off in the texts. That was the painful part. It seemed everyone was relaxed from the tension of learning and now we had to ramp up, back at it. We were quickly rousted from a shroud of tranquility which later reminded me of the beginning of the film *Dr Zhivago*. Cold winter storm, very young adolescent, window looking out to a frozen land, adult happenings surrounding, cocooned under the warm covers of a long winter's night not sure what the morning would bring except the cold. War was on the horizon and we didn't know it.

This book is dedicated to Rick Pierce from Grant High School 1966, a friend, who didn't make it back home from war. Most everyone in the Portland high schools experienced similar memories as a kid growing up in the 50's and early 60's. Life blossomed with the tunes and songs of Fats Domino, the Beach Boys, Jan and Dean and Louie Louie. My generation shall never forget all the athletic, hormonal, academic, and parental frustrations heaped on us that we experienced to a very full measure.

Vietnam shattered our childhood fantasies. We were no longer naive to the world's way. We were part of it, in some cases to the death. As a generation we carry the deep scars of a society out of control as the generations before us in Korea and WWII, except Vietnam was different. It was a war that either a young man wanted to wear the uniform or was too poor to go to college and had to bear the uniform. Most who fought the war were too poor to avoid the draft.

We became part of the legacy of crazy men on the other side of the world. Our own crazy men in charge of our lives participated in return. It took me a lifetime to turn to poetry as a sublime way to appreciate the finest of who we are.

The moment of the Twenty-One Gun salute at Willamette National Cemetery in 1967 memorializing LCP Merrick Pierce, shocked the underpinnings of my life. Those who attended, his family, other friends, and fellow soldiers appeared to have been deeply affected by the funeral rite. Approaching the Oregon Vietnam War Memorial and The Wall in Washington DC is difficult. Everyone else who has grieved shares the same internal anguish and outward sad traumatic disquiet. It ought not to have happened the way it did; history that is.

AUTHOR PREFACE

The reckoning of who we are is a composite of our indelible past images we call history, and our future which is what we are about to learn from peering into the expanse of the Universe visualizing all we can be.

To get to our future we have a choice. We can see ourselves as small marbles vibrating on a table in motion from some force we don't understand or care about as we live our lives empty and ineffectual, unable to collect ourselves into any cohesion from separate parts, rolling and colliding about at random. Or, we can gather the parts of ourselves into a contiguous whole and merge with our future as it unfolds, directing our personal energies toward acquiring within a Socratic Virtue.

The choice seems clear. We can move through the Threshold in front of us by moving one step into and through the perceived difficulty, only to find there was no pain to the experience.

Our biology is the cause of wars. Our minds and what is within us cause our future. Again, we can explore and attempt to understand the Universe investing our minds and five senses, or be a species meandering aimlessly until the next unintended consequence of a random occurrence.

FOREWARD

This volume, *Thresholds*, a compendium of poems by Douglas W Anderson is the fifth and most satisfying effort by the author who has been engaged for the last fifteen years in the stimulation and exploration of his own creativity. I gather from conversations with him that it has been an arduous albeit meaningful journey. As he says in his comments "The most difficult aspect of writing poetry is to expose the personal self."

Dr. Anderson, who I met early in my own academic career, had a long and successful career as an academic anesthesiologist. It may help the reader to understand something about that life. The world and mental state in which an anesthesiologist must operate occupies a very different terrain from that of the creative writer. Training to become an expert in this field involves investing wholly, and fully, all of one's mental and physical energy for a decade, forgoing the pleasures, avocations, and pursuits that others are free to pursue in their 20's. This training process results in doctors with a deep understanding of human physiology, pharmacology, and procedures who are able to shepherd patients safely through surgeries using drugs that, if miscalculated or misused, can surely kill. Anesthesiologists routinely bring patients into and out of "the valley of death." This is not a creative process. It is bound by protocols tested by the adamantine methods of science and requires constant focused attention to assure the safety of patients. The mental state and processes of creating poetry could not be more different and it is a remarkable accomplishment to be successful in both.

The poems in *Thresholds* vary in theme, length, and timbre. Some in the second section of the book, "Thoughts about War" will resonate very deeply with members of my generation who grew up with the Vietnam War. *Thresholds* is dedicated to Rick Pierce, a high school friend of the author who lost his life in Vietnam. The many casualties from that war did not cease when the last American troops left Saigon in 1975. A close friend of mine from high school, afflicted with PTSD, retreated to a life of isolation in the Alaskan wilderness. Another friend died, shot by police in the midst of a flashback. Memories activated by these lines in "The Dinner Table:"

> "...seeing the images of a soldier's helmet.
> chin straps hanging down beside
> their ears so the shock of a bullet,
> did not rip their head off when struck,
> wearing uniforms that didn't fit,
> sleeves rolled up because of the heat
> and humidity without any benefit"

will bring some of us back to those times and may enable younger generations a window into the experience of their elders. My father was a Marine in the Pacific during WWII who never talked about his experiences in the war. I never really understood what he went through until I saw The Pacific, the HBO series. Often, it is only the visual and literary arts that can communicate experiences to which we have no personal access.

Dr. Anderson explores many aspects of war and conflict deeply in these poems introducing this section of the collection with "The Coffee Bean Essay" a thought experiment reflecting on the importance of cooperation to survival and referencing obliquely the field of game theory on which much of modern war strategy rests (Steinhaus, Hugo (1949). "The problem of fair division" *Econometrica*.17: 315–9). The longest poem "The Manifest Destiny of War" is an exploration of the individual and cultural determinants of war and its threat to our survival as a species. Subsequent poems describe the horror of the battlefield ("Distant Thunder"), our vulnerability to annihilation due to the madness of our leaders ("The Turn of Nuclear Events"), inculturation to conflict "The Culture of War"), the contribution of religion to war ("A Religious Belief"), and the relation of the individual's internal struggles to external conflict ("Conflict Within")

"The war within themselves seeks a way out
to fight the war aspired to, and the continued war within
cannot accept defeat because of the heart's darkness"

Two poems ("Finding a Mate" and "Another Origin of Conflict") touch on the theme of sexual competition as a genesis of conflict and an intriguing poem in the first section of the book ("Helen of Troy") muses on the most famous story of war precipitated by these passions as told in Homer's *Iliad*. Some of Dr. Anderson's poetry carries the same power of evocation as images in that ancient text.

From "Distant Thunder":

"...or perhaps at sunset where the gas
rolls slow over the fields of burnt cinders
blackened skeletons and pocked surfaces,
coming to inflict a quick death."

And from the *Iliad*:
"...but there they lay, sprawled across the field, craved far more by the vultures than by wives."

There is much in the first section of the book, "Thoughts and Observations", that will intrigue the reader as well. A stanza in the poem "Politics or Science" conjures memories of Plato's *Allegory of the Cave*.

"Ours is a field of tall tassels, flowing, moving with the wind,
never actually seeing the wind to identify shapes.
The wind contours the undulant tufted surface tassels
in an illusion appearing to be alluring and stunning"

This collection of poems explores many of the dark corners of human existence but always with a leavening of hope that we can overcome our frailties, survive, and prosper. The final poem in the book, "Our Possibility", gives this sentiment explicit voice.

"War is our single part once eliminated,
will allow us to survive."

Reading these poems will require effort and contemplation from the reader. This is always the case with meaningful poetry since each person must incorporate the words, images, and thoughts into their own experience and individual meaning. Those who take up the challenge will be rewarded with their own personal exploration of these ideas.

George A. Keepers, M.D.
Professor and Chair, Department of Psychiatry
Oregon Health & Science University

CONTENTS

Author Preface   13

Foreword   15

Part I Thoughts and Observations   21

In the Beginning   23
Destiny Transforms Life   25
Politics or Science   27
Empathy   29
In a Dark Place   31
Two Types of People   34
White from Blue   36
The Seat   38
Empty Room   40
The Devil's House   41
The Law   44
Dwelling (Temple-Place)   45
The Problem with Induction   46
Language, Silence and Mortar   47
King Arthurs' Allegory   49
Dark Blood Dark Matter   51
The Delusion, Illusion and Conflict   56
Chance Occurrence   58
Ελένη (Helen) of Troy   60
Never More Than   62
Thresholds   64
Neuroprotection   67
Evil   68
The Political Event   70

The Governors Choice	72
Alone	74
Afterlife	76
An Idea in Stone	77
Jesus or Shi	79
The Contours of Fate	81
To Slow Time	82
In Memory of Betty	83
The Final Roll Call	84
To Read the Masters	86

Part II Thoughts About War — 87

The Coffee Bean Essay	89
The Manifest Nature of War	91
Notes	98
Distant Thunder	100
A Warring Strategy	101
The Turn of Nuclear Events	102
A Bad Dream	103
The Culture of War	104
Finding a Mate	105
A Religious Belief	106
Conflict Within	109
Competition for Resources	111
The Dinner Table	112
Another Origin of Conflict	114
War as an Outgrowth of Culture	115
Memories of Growing Up	116
The Making of a Disturbed Person	119
The Making of a Disturbed Soldier	121
War is in the Heart of Man	122
Our Possibility	127
About the Author	129

Part I Thoughts and Observations

In the Beginning

There is a time late at night,
when the moon is full and bright,
therein is cast only the moonlight,
where no shadow exists in sight.

Straight from above in the night sky,
no penetrating ray detected from nigh,
only the reflection from a frosted lanai,
an appearance of the fallow colors reply.

Intrepid moments aroused and awakened,
from sleep and dreams eyes sharpened,
feeling a quick reality of being summoned,
akin to a spiritual anxiety rechristened.

In my earliest childhood moments,
staring between my bedroom valence,
the moonlight shown then a transience,
of equal effect as last night's silence.

My spiritual journey began alone,
in the second story window zone,
where there were no shadows overtone,
on the street's quiet moonstone.

An acceptance of peace inside was untied,
although the Gordian Knot still exemplified
some strain of belief and denial dignified.
It began the beginning of a magnified divide.

In time the scene above was so inclusive,
the awakening so spiritual and cognitive,
the repeating of it over time suggestive,
that it be examined in the reclusive.

So, life's process was the journey chosen!

Destiny Transforms Life

If you believe in destiny as a means
of perfecting emotions of love,
then we have come to a union;
a deep commitment achieved.
Living life that is not a betrayal,
to ourselves or of another's love,
is an attractive affirmation,
as intense feelings surface.
These are rare moments
to witness coming to light.

The allusion is ours to dream,
but a sharing of illusions in everyday life,
holds little promise of spiritual union.
The illusions are measured,
in a nurturing stepwise ascent.
The requisites of living from
day to day in a commitment,
close to the heart and secure,
offers little intimate connection,
with an apparent destined fate.

When we sought refuge,
apart from the impelling powers,
our sanctuary was just big enough,
for us to caress into one body.
We sustained our merged shape,
quivering, embracing our souls,
uniting our hearts life blood,
with spiritual certainty,
one but not one,
as I am with you,
as you are with me.

A life destined traveling toward the sun,
into a radiant shape there is cast a small,
but luminous shadow, as if to leave behind,
an innocence untouched by any constraint,
to live and love the remarkable life.
Once fate's expected emotions,
are expressed with patience and perfection,
ignited by the sun's blaze of ecstasy,
a destiny is shaped into a life,
of an unknown power and celerity.

Politics or Science

If you land on the moon step down on the surface
and just disappear, poof, we should try again.
If you land on the moon again stepping down
on the surface and suddenly, poof, gone again,
would that be the politics of it all or the science ignored?

We still mix the two even at the limits of earth,
thinking our house is without a faulty joist.
Many try to keep this threshold from our reality.
So far, so good they say?

Ours is a lot we seem to not be able to change,
the politics of budget, position, unspiritual,
the ego of marginal safety, the infamous smoking cigar,
feet on the desk, reusable parts, when to replace.

We should be wary of taking the risks.
We should be weary of praying for those
so bold who have faith in our science.

What course correction or new paradigm should we
conceive to imagine the mindfulness we may tender,
other than the terra firma dust to dust usual preference,
in case the unforeseen or abrupt happens?

The left behind or the forever in motion,
enlarging their orbital eccentricity or reentry,
leaves no evidence to mandate how we should change.
Perhaps we already know?

Ours is a field of tall tassels, flowing, moving with the wind,
never actually seeing the wind to identify shapes.
The wind contours the undulant tufted surface tassels,
in an illusion appearing to be alluring and stunning,

compelling us between constant motion and stillness,
always trying to make the integral a perfect curve,
always trying to remove the decision errors,
electing instead the programmer and computer.

Empathy

You have made clear your view and perspective,
that which is limited in focus and knowledge base.
Do you have another perspective I can listen to?
Can you step into a new framework?
Can you turn ninety degrees with as much enthusiasm,
as you display in your current delivery?

I also look for some nonlinear thoughts,
expressed as essential prior knowledge,
you deem important in an associative context.
For example, I think it important to understand
"The Iliad" as an example of how war wreaks
damage upon the solder, commander, and enemy.

The poem, two weeks of history, 2700 years ago,
is as essential as The Red Badge of Courage today.
They are the episteme of war, acts and effects of war not doxa.
We learn that war is the act of distant and close killing,
its effects on empathy as a dying part of us,
unable to connect to our goodness in this world.

You also speak about the successes of other beliefs.
My western world has been a success in many ways too.
There are always failures in any culture, ours included.
Supporting within any realm despotism and subjugation
of half the human race no matter who they are,
owing to the whims of a hierarchy are two such failures.

When I can no longer believe in the Apostles' Creed,
or the original Nicene Creed as literal dogma of faith,
I would be in a faith crisis hurrying to find perhaps,
a solution within my community of similar beliefs.
These acts would require a turning of sorts,
exposing my knowledge in all its flaws and certainties.

Can we talk about empathy as a cultural deficit?
We own enough blame to go around!
Or better, cite a pathway to an individual or
cultural empathy within our ethical sea.
We could seek points from several perspectives!
Please show me as you turn your many sides!

Presently I see many blank spots, deficits.
Please, what are you doing about them?
I don't know where I learned to turn in motion,
perhaps when I was very young having friends,
who often were spinning sadness and rejection.
Many in the world today have nurtured empathy.

Can you?

In a Dark Place

Todd Milledge DDS
1963 - 2015

We all bear some substance of a dark place,
wherein there was no light at times to see clear.
However, to see makes no difference when
self-deception moves one alone to a final act.
For us who are left to bury the dead,
the image is burned into memory forever.

The time is neither a moment nor an hour.
The day is neither light nor leaden.
The night is neither dark nor star-lit,
calm or engaged.

All images are colorless,
an inveterate gray.

The cloud of impending choice
rains a calm shower to start.
The cold drops stop for just awhile.
The cold shimmering remnants of a life,
begin to come apart and separate,
piece by piece.
The deed is about to be done.

The setting is in a dark place, unnoticed,
one life, unable to get beyond the first thought.

The descent is:
one thought,
an experiment at first,
then resignation,
submission,
freedom,
concealment,
commitment,
the time of moment,
arising from preparation and impulse.

A time lapse no matter the time taken.
All in a mixture heading for a point,
only to be buried in the earth,
perhaps eventually removed from memory.
There is a deep disturbance in the souls
of those who saw it coming in hindsight.
Into the abyss fall the emotions of those who didn't.

Who is left?
Those thinking they could have helped,
or some who saw the pattern in hindsight?
There are many in mourning who will carry the visage,
not in fragmented pieces, but whole images of the past,
perhaps over a lifetime.
The news is a painful defeat of
everyone's humanity stirring within.
Our Guide did not prepare us for the loss?

Those living with the absence,
see the act as having broken,
with the faith of life.

The living stay connected.
They can get beyond the first thought.
They can see in a dark place.

So, look among you now.
Find those who are open to be loved.
In a dark place,
they will always see light.

When we touch our inner soul appears.
When we look into the eyes of another,
what is revealed emerges gentle,
a vitality and promise of life,
embedded in the source of belief,
a belief in ourselves so we can see.
This will always get us
past the first thought.

Turning to say I Love You,
will always get us past fear,
to allow the second thought.

To see the Sun shine from a dark place,
to feel the warm rays of life,
all we have to do is look up,
to our life giver,

an impulse of affirmation.

Two Types of People

There are two types of people.
The reproductive aspects will
take care of themselves,
except about how the children
are nourished and educated.

The first type want housing
and food provided over time;
only the Government to own land.
The second type want
to build their own house and grow
their own food on their own land.

The neurocircuitry of one,
understands the other.
It only goes one way!
One is free and the other,
would like to be free.

Life goes two ways!
Either fear pretending to know,
with anger as a front to behavior,
or knowledge, with courage to move
into the future as the Earth ages.

Independence represented to one,
is threatening and tenebrous;
much safer to be led, fed, and nurtured,
serving the masters, winning,
ambitious to control.

Independence to the other,
represents freedom and clarity;
to be free in thought and deed.

We were born alone and will die alone.
In between we have a choice.
Taking that choice is doing who we are,
either to live life or be ruled by those
who would like us to fall as prey.

White from Blue

For Alexa Maria
Tú eres de mí como el blanco es del azul.
(You are from me as white is from blue.)

A Mexican baptism is the struggle between the demon-snake
stealing the soul of the baby and the redemption from the original sin.

White on blue an infant and mother's hue,
colors of the baptism dresses new.
You are from me, white from blue,
the first mustērion for original sin rescue.

An affusion baptism from the goblet,
where salvation arises working implicit,
in the name of cleansing original sin explicit,
the Trinity, Father, Son, and Holy Spirit.

Signs of grace from Christ, the sacrament,
invested by the Church*, a necessary element,
by which divine life, its portended precedent,
is granted to one proclaiming the gospel invariant.

Initiation to a rite of passage, an entrance transformation,
to be reborn, is a relief from impious histories origination.
The sacred histories begin anew of Gods' creation,
through the power of the priest and Apostolic succession.

Upon the lifting arms of godparents, she ascends,
the temporal life drops away, a child's initiation commends
into the life of the children of God, Ex opere operato transcends.
Baptism Peter's way into the Spirit where God endures, we send.

Quetzalcoatl was born of a virgin.
Priests were wearing wind jewels over faces wizened.
Catholics were suffused with myth legends,
preaching one god where four winds leavened,

assimilating the sacrificial heart communion,
and the midwife rituals, water, words, and blood infusion,
exorcising the spirit that dwelled in the serpent crucifixion,
and the poison inherent in a quest for liberation.

The four cardinal points covered with oil and ceremony,
the fiery signal completes the circle of history,
the bird, the serpent, heaven and earth in harmony,
the river of sins never washed the four winds in captivity.

In accordance, an unbaptized child's fate is uncertain.
Alexa's future lies in the body temporal and spiritual union.
The woman her mother is, will guide this ceremony unbroken,
into her future loves, friendships, family ties, and succession.

White on blue an infant and mother's hue,
colors of the baptism dresses new.
You are from me, white from blue,
you love me, I love you.

* St Juan Diego Parish, Cowiche, WA

The Seat

You look extant,
rigid, oblique, hard, self-protective,
not to be approached to close.
Perhaps a seat next to you
would not be too close,
or otherwise,
take the chance!
Oops, the buttocks moved a bit!

You appear hidden within,
a glass bubble about to crack.
Say hello to your countenance,
missing the mirrored mark.

A nod reply was expressionless,
looking into a book,
whose title was of course, fiction.

All things important emigrated from you,
as you lifted your gaze in a moment,
and looked above everyone,
then your eyes set again onto the pages.
Arrogance oozed,
rejecting that which was around you,
instead of receiving.

It is difficult to penetrate,
that kind of carbon sheet steel.

You were clearly suspicious of me.
None of this was lost on you getting to be,
the first on the airplane.

I just wanted to sit down,
because my back was sore!

Empty Room

Without people the room is empty.
It remains empty until,
people fill the room.
It could be empty forever.
It looks that way now,
dark, silent, still, stale.

But people are transient,
only to fill the room,
once in a while.
Also, it is more than once in a while,
the room remains empty,
for longer times than full.

The empty room is also transient.
It is a boundless circle,
temporarily expanding into,
a finite cubic dimension,
the form we give this space.

The form is real though,
only because we perceive it such.
Otherwise, it is only substance,
recycled atoms from the eternal pulsing
of, perhaps, many Big Bangs.

Life is the only part of the universe
to give reality meaning.

The next step of this process,
is to be curious and understand,
how this can be so!

The Devil's House*

*For Chris, Tom, Heather,
Sarahlee, Morgan, Katie, and Laura*

*I have met the Devil, and stayed two weeks in his house.
(The Grand Canyon*, The Colorado River)*

*In a spirit quest a life force will enter into you.
When you have manifested your introversion journey
your soul will have spoken to you. Accepting "Nature" as is,
is the first encounter of spirituality, which will become many,
traveling the way, merging the philosopher, scientist, and artist.*

Nature is.
It is neutral to either/or if assigned a perception.
The five senses transmute it as discrete, unholy.
In the end we are crushed by its gravity,
to be reformed as ice or matter perhaps,
exploded into the universe as darkness.

DNA's velocity will surely stop.
The central elements of our chemistry,
are only held captive for a while.
In the end nothing will exist as we know it.
Our Guide promised us a sublime departure.
Our spiritual existence is only a parable,
secure in who we are while alive,
a contrived bit of excellence within our humanity.

In the Devil's House we come face to face
with the feeling of what is possible to face,
the remnants of the slabs of hardened time,
the limestone chards laying where they fell,
skeletons with arms folded, legs crossed,
reclining in the slanted inguinal form, poised,
still immovable, heavy, in a terminus position.

There is a layer of relief just above the water,
cool flowing air relieving the fire of heat,
evaporating, evaporating, evaporating,
your skin merging with the brown sand.
No monuments explicit except the Canyon,
a deep fissure of tectonic slow rising and falling.

The weathering of course one cannot witness.
The limestone blocks of sparkling polished
gray and blackness are results of time,
ancient perhaps, but one never knows.
They could have been placed yesterday,
by the providence of just a stone's fall.

The water is green below Glen Canyon,
brown is the color we see at the end,
a journey in witness to constant change,
remembering Heraclitus with each step,
sharing the water with ants, geckos,
and the occasional Willet at water's edge.

The Devil's House is one we enter into
from time to time,
no one lives in this house though.
It is always changing into and forming,
completing any transformation before
we reach to touch the entrance,
that place we enter into through the door.

There are no mood changes as one
moves down river until Separation Canyon,
when you witness the water cut visual,
that may last for a thousand years.
We make no difference to the gods,
the ones who have power to move stones and rocks,
that measure time through the millennia.

The massive beauty of Nature's being is,
and contrived in the thought we give it reality.
The Devil's House is the flux of form, flowing outward,
we want so much to be still and see as still.
It only persists and alters in a long length of time,
under the watch of canyon walls and the Milky Way.

The Law

Settling a dispute, always some part of a lie,
expressed by others, or stated by yourself,
little or substantial, is a judgment affair.
Don't ever underestimate the power of the banal,
to explain the complex, and reduce the truth,
to a simplistic level, to act and render, a judgment.
In spite of what you witness, "Justice" then happens,
as the essential dispute stakes a position as truth;
a Sisyphean influence of a Sisyphean condition.

Temple (Dwelling)   *Ναός (Κατοικία)*

There is a stark clarity or openness
between the cornerstone and the sky.
A sanctum, once appearing to stand forever,
has been forgotten through history long ago;
even the rubble has been cleaned away.
Brown grass grows between cut stones.

The leveled foundation and queued columns,
stand in repute to a lost deity who was truth.
The ground is hard compressed by centuries.
All shapes in the eye's perusal appear weighted.
A précis sky and sun confer tragedy at noon,
unlike night when peace and sleep are vulnerable.

A constant wind profiles the undulate landscape,
drying the notched domain over the millennia,
preserving what remains of a myth underlying
orisons and what endured from the past.

This isolated place was meant to be remote.
The small temple facing east had meaning,
to those who searched for the unconcealed
thread of ordinary mysteries and existence,
setting in motion interest that turned inward.

Their work, form, fabric, invention, oeuvre,
are all gone except fragments of composition.
Their dust has been mixed with millennial grit,
that polished the surfaces of the laid stones,
raised in the tradition of Heraclitus and Pericles.

The Problem with Induction

Induction suggests truth, as uncertain as that is,
in the minds of those who don't know
what may be false in the face of appearing true.

If the organ systems of all adults
appear healthy from questions and answers,
then all adults are OK to undergo anesthesia.

If the child's heart, health and lack of syndromes,
appear healthy from questions and answers,
then all children are OK to undergo anesthesia.

Induction competitiveness with Reason,
displays ignorance and the potential of reality.
It may express the certainty of a false conclusion.

Ergo, the predictive power only goes so far,
when the qualified give way and accept,
the unqualified as qualified to display mastery.

Language, Silence and Mortar

When you hear someone speak,
what do you hear?
When you read a biography,
what do you see in your mind's eye?
When language engages you to think
what do your thoughts reveal to you?
Even the Primal Call opens thoughts,
but may obstruct coherence as abscesses
from the heart are voiced pouring forth.

When we read we envision and sense.
Possibly we should do that more often.
What does language assert about us?
Perhaps we should just fall silent
on occasion to lessen the barriers
that confront us using language.
It is more often listening to
our primal nature and falling silent,
that unfurls us to openness.

We are set in the Earth
from birth through death.
We are alive breathing the ether
for the time we dwell under the stars.
We worship our God as we evolve
with time, as the image changes
of ourselves and our language.
We as Mortals in time die.

We posit the difference
between us and the gods,
between us and our God,
between openness and concealment,
between belief, truth and our nature,
as the balancing of our mortary makeup.

King Arthurs' Allegory

Guinevere has the power of the feminine,
almost unknowable to the masculine.
Arthur has the power of the masculine,
knowable to the feminine.

In the quiet of the forest,
a virginal tree pure of heartwood,
draws a maidenly life from within.
Its chaste reserve sets forth the birth
of a moral creation eventually
transcending masculine virtues.

The birth of altering the powerful begins
with a life of apparent weakness.

Arthur must follow her insight,
drawn to the supreme seduction,
in the course of settling Saxon battles,
or conflict among themselves,
Pelagian, in defense of free will.

The gods are sure she is poised,
to know something of the legions,
to know something of the powerful.
The biology is different, disparate,
a basic conflict, discrete, divergent.

She knows something that
gives her courage to emanate
a Christian power to rule men,
an instinct of scent, seduction,
a tack, way, using parables,
allegories, morality, redolent of
ancient myths and mysteries.

To cause the course of history
to bend from the masculine
and secular toward a regeneration
of myth, peace and protection,
contrary to the sword of battle,
is distinct and different; natures' way.

The bonds of love and power,
are rooted in the feminine.
Guinevere and Lancelot's betrayal
is deeply rooted in original sin and forgiveness,
syncretized with imperfect innate human goodness.

The master in the cloak and mask,
the masculine is seated as king.
Christian virtue and power, the true sovereign,
is seated adjacent in the guise of the feminine.

The weakness and strength of the masculine in history,
is the strength and weakness of the feminine in history.

Dark Blood Dark Matter

Our origins were out of mother Africa,
into the future breadbasket of Mesopotamia,
migrating outward beyond mountains and seas,
over the world with no boundaries,
four points of direction,
thousands of years ago.

We posited matrices here and there,
some were contingent, some flourished,
some emerged, some perished unknown,
some built civilizations, expiating a trail
of Dark Blood and bones.

The largest of these mass migrations,
African-Indo-European, Eurasian to
North and South America and Great Atlantic,
displacements and expansionism are over.
Six continents it was, rich in resources,
countless wars of imposition immorality,
levying a price of exultation and tragedy,
the way and manner of science and God,
the vanquished buried under the footings.

The empire gleams in the sun.
Time is obscured to a patient pretender.
Culture waxes to tribalism and surrender.
Mythology wanes to something factual.
Witches cast spells emulating empathy.

Who is next in the modern world,
expanding in a mass migration?
When dawn clarifies the night images,
of the mountains, prairies, rivers and oceans,
which ground will ignite a new genesis;
where shall it come from?

Could it be as great as those migrations,
over the Savannah so few in numbers,
or the travails through Beringian borders,
or those to the terminus south?

At least half the world is still open,
or are we so near our neighbor and resolute,
the doors we might step through to change,
might be closed to any emergence?
When shall it come?
Just look over the horizon.
Is there a new origin to know?

Knowing carries a burden of a special case.
Nothing can be altered for the outcome.
The last door to open to see into infinity is,
mass migrations occur, Nature is.
The forward velocity of DNA is sure.
Consciousness is obscure in all prism colors.
Our shadow holds us back from the sublime.

Not knowing we should blame ourselves.
But knowing, since asking questions,
should reveal our comprehension;
peoples will be venerated peoples will be oppressed.

The Origins and Will shall testify to be,
but shall be resolutely compressed,
and politically driven unlike the original Origins.
No millennia will shape it, just compressed pressure,
to move from fear and want of the hearts measure,
unlike the evolved genus Homo, over time.

Causation is what the historians think it is,
from selection of facts over the studied time.
The colors are gray, dirty water, and brown earth;
a Malthusian curve describes the abstract truth.
Mass movements are sure, never static, always moving,
appearing to settle, but only for a time.
There are no fences that hold humans in,
only fear that keeps us from getting out.

Governments are evil and malign mass movements,
eyes closed, silent tongues, open mouths,
breathing their beliefs deep into everyone.
Despots like Stalin and Mao defined a new meaning
of death viewed the human train as waste tallies,
letting the future bury them in deep valleys,
far from their birth lands scarred with death pyres,
all focused and perpetrated again by modern War Lords.

From the time of Heraclitus, even before,
when the gods were a pantheon of lore,
in a shared hierarchy of polytheism,
to the gods we have today, and allegories believed as fact,
never have mass migrations been stopped or abated,
that emanate from the psyche of the human spirit,
to the ends of the conquered and vanquished.

For those seeking food, shelter,
and reproduction with the sword,
they shall be the blessed in the eye
of the disappearing vanquished,
whose molecules and atoms return
to the earth base of carbon and silicon,
eventually streaking as times arrow,
in faint flight to and through Dark Matter.
Who will read the inscriptions on the cenotaphs,
and ruins of both conquerors and vanquished,
who end up in the buried sands of times mortar?

Surely, we have come to the end of this time,
facing a future without any god to pray to,
discovering gravitational waves in other galaxies,
hurling ourselves from one Monad to another,
holding our future in a weakened psychological grasp,
hoping for a transcendence with no preparation,
trying to weave the fabric of our future mythology.

The psyche of the human spirit is only a promise to our self.
Consciousness may have been a mistake of our essential nature.
Self-awareness may have been an ultimate form of destruction,
in our quest for understanding and harnessing fusion.
There can be no Judeo-Christian sentiment
in delusional madness, just the loss of an epoch.
Looking inward or outward makes no difference to Nature.
Nature is conceived in the sublime of our intellect, indifferent to us.
Eventually our ashes follow the existence of the Sun.

Looking at Earth from Cassini, we have nowhere else to go.
The blue orb color is light reflected outward off Earths' surface.
The origin is the fusion of nuclei stripped of electrons in the Sun.
It radiates outward lighting our present and future way.

We have learned nothing from our past when light has guided us,
to the place we now know; our faith has been alleged an allegory.
Trying as we may have, whether we promise ourselves anything,
we cannot convince nature to accept us as if it was not indifferent,
nor can Nature, Time and Space sense anything.

Time to look inward to our godhead.
Allegories and parables have already shown the way.
Our sense of justice is obscured in thought and act,
blinded, it does not equate fair and reasonable in a dispute.
The act of justice alone belies any sense of right.

Mass migrations are the way of our species,
inherent in the sinews of our pneuma,
beyond modern inventions of nation states,
beyond governments social contract with citizens,
not dependent on tribalism for movement,
but inborn and congenital at birth at least,
up to the transfiguration point of death.

Mass migrations spawn new mysteries,
in allegories of mythology which is always
a changing conflict with the constant,
arising within the deep cultural fabric in each of us;
newly conceived concepts of justice and mercy,
without which any empire will meet its demise.
The contradiction is always ever present!

The Delusion, Illusion and Conflict   *A Trinity*

The delusion starts with the father.
He sees his son growing similar to his future.
The illusion starts with the son.
He lives for the future he seeks.

As the son learns and grows a conflict ensues,
causing his belief plans to be delayed,
as he pursues a higher education,
necessarily separating with the father.

The son becomes humbled knowing nothing,
he seeks a better quality of information.
Thus, begins a disciplined inquiry.
The father waits for his own image to be realized.

The son's ego dies challenging knowledge.
He becomes the master of the learning process,
so that he will not be shamed.
The father becomes reluctant to accept the process.

The son becomes an ascetic purifying his body,
denying the body pleasures for the while.
The nature of his first Karmic contract,
will force him to make a change though.

There are many father expectations and desires
in his mind, consequent to an understanding.
There are son expectations of enlightenment,
oneness with everything, an identity of harmony.

Jesus was anointed,
Buddha attained enlightenment.
There are two ways to unravel reality,
reward in the occidental is afterlife;
reward in the oriental is in life.

Chance Occurrence

Life is a chance occurrence, death is certain.
To master and reinforce personal confidence,
or effectance is principal to be vital.

All life tends toward death.
What eras are over for us?
What eras are beginning for us?
Consciousness is the only era interval of being.

The rest of any time span is a consequence,
of looking at a watch or calendar,
imagining the merged carnal and spiritual
content of an idea before the continuum of dust.

Being alive we have a choice.
To be free or be led.
If free we will have conflict.
If led we will have conflict.

For those who will be led in any manner,
many will possess strife against us.
The others may actually be free in form,
thinking there is a benevolent King.
Some may attain Freedom and Liberty yet alienated.

Animosity in all forms does rain,
over those who are Free.
It is like a pendulum's amplitude;
what is certain to manifest, is.

The best place to be is the frictionless pivot,
the rest will only know a trajectory,
many will never know equilibrium,
none will know about the restoring force.

Their feelings projected on those who
are free within will cause loss of heart.
Their heart is already austere.

Life is a chance occurrence.
Nature is!

Religion can only try to suspend the is.
It convinces one to dissolve
into the community of sameness.
Look at the effect with a conspicuous perspective.

We are judgmental about ourselves.
The manifesto helps guide us to perdition,
disguised as the ostensible heaven.
We, perforce, our allegiance from within.

The conflict is poison to all.
We live in the milieu of what we created.
So many could and will follow or obey.
So many will reproduce, emanate and succeed.

Life is a chance occurrence!
Death is certain.
More certain than what we do,
to ourselves in any color of expression.

Ελένη (Helen) of Troy

Helen was a compelling force in History,
Woven into the sinews of Time,
and the Synapses of our Mythology

Helen, Selene, torch light, infecund, Venus,
Sun Goddess, progenitor of prurient desire,
arising from under the Bronze Age aegis,
of the gods only to transform and transpire.

The myth resting for a time in allegory,
changing character forms to procreate,
which god or mortal shall tell the story,
beginning the process of Helens fate?

Fathered by Zeus whose impersonate Swan form,
wrapped a cuckold Leda with a sensitive force,
repeating his intromission and rapacious perform,
with a god's disguise as men's delusions of intercourse.

Leda continuing her perversity yielded to Tyndareus,
in his bed that night congruent with a husband's mortality,
giving birth eventually to two eggs both bloodless.
Twins hatched semi divine and mortal, four fated in mythology.

Helen was beautiful as pubescence can reflect.
In time Theseus desired her with thoughts of seduction,
worthy of how women were valued as an object,
hiding her away having his way over her dominion.

Helen was rescued and brought home without coercion,
The suiters took the oath of Tyndareus and she married Menelaus,
to be part of the god's folly and coxcomb seduction,
by the very Paris and Olympian inveigled deceiver coyness.

Penetration is dominant during moments of seduction and ravish,
the genesis of the inveterate adulation of sexual empowerment.
The myth imposes on Helen a splendor to many would be anguish,
ageing under Priam's eye a discursive feminine eventually less ardent.

After the sack of Troy Helen rejoins Menelaus at Sparta.
Shame over time is forgiven in his sanctuary as she receives her master.
Clytemnestra rails about the sacrifice of Helens daughter Iphigenia,
a ritual death to entice the Hellenic winds on to the plain of Scamander.

Hermione was smothered in Hellenic genealogy only to disappear.
Helen is a force of history woven into time as is vulcanism and tsunamis,
into the historical roars of thunder at the end of the Minoan era,
in our eschatology within the evolution of our deities and fancies.

Helen was whisked to Mt Olympus before her moment of demise,
dressed in her Challis at the god's nexus who made her semi mortal at birth.
We live today the fecund and beauty myth all men wish to fantazise,
the prospect of fertility and rights to the ancient chattel men desire of worth.

Never More Than

When you, with others, exist in trust,
they may prey upon you at some time.
For them redemption matters not.

Perhaps in turn you will betray them.
Your ensuing self-redemption will never
make you whole in human spirit.
Your self-quest will perhaps get you close.
For them, a quest matters not.

For you, trust may become a life's journey,
perpetually to repeat in your Place.
For them, empathy is weakness.
For them, they fear their last breath.

For me, I live through my breathing,
and struggle with the hostile wrest,
between the spiritual and temporal worlds,
while balancing time and space in league,
with the resonant polarity of a poem.

We always try to restructure time,
distressing to be whole in the emotional chaos,
before our spirit energy explodes,
into the universe free from time,
where the event horizon supplants the atom.

In our venue we exist as part of the whole,
where poetry has freed us from pain.
Chronos will cease at an event horizon,
where we will end in infinity as nuclei,
where the song is silenced and mute.

Having manifested myself with breathing,
as this vessel has coalesced with my spirit,
it is the quest to exist in trust with others,
that has defined within me the difference,
between a Place and a place.

Thresholds

The truth is hidden behind many layers,
easily unfolding when we think in other perspectives.
The doors and thresholds that confront us,
often change our view as we peer into ourselves.

The doors are always open.
It is the thresholds that hold fast.
They restrain our spirit from engaging,
an entry in a time of pronouncement.

Over a lifetime how long one lives,
to be able to convene the truth,
to pledge a covenant or discernment,
depends on the worsening of the disease.

The truth about this is never easy.
The truth is harder than denial.
We end when the time comes,
still confronting an unknown threshold.

Speak to the rock.
It has form.
It is art and is,
as still as it sets.

The art we seek is truth unconcealed.
It can be the thread that connects,
the love of sentiment,
open to human touch,
serving only one master.

The light from an open door
invites a world of any age,
never affected by Chronos,
open to Causality facets,
both past and future.

We are sometimes summoned
to watch the moons lunar cycle,
from light to dark and by torchlight,
giving birth to the sun and dawn,
coveted by the "eye of the night,
queen among stars…" *

You can look into the sun,
follow the lure of the sky,
sense the changing light,
gathering prism colors.

Set foot in the river,
trace the arrows flight,
watch your shadow
following you in the light.

The shade form may reshape,
but not its substance.
It is always there,
part of your darkness.
Let it be as is.

Sanctify the soil you walk upon.
Take its nourishment past the entrance.
It will sustain your quiet passage,
from the night's dream tension.

Whether Orient or Occident,
the way of the mystic,
should expose your
highest sublime potential,
to cross thresholds.

The door is always clear to passage.
It is the night and the thresholds,
that have force of immanence,
or noumenal significance.

The morning doors are aligned
with the thresholds step.
The nights reprieve is only a waiting
for the release of fear,
or any consequent affirmation.

* *The Seven Plays in English Verse,*
   (Seven Against Thebes) by Aeschylus

Neuroprotection

What neuroprotection do you recruit,
to resist against the cerebral factions,
the dissenters of reason emerging from
schisms and chasms terracing a couloir,
nurturing upward to defile even the seculars?

Yes, the conspirators who purely believe
their Byzantine presence is pleasant.
They possess no empathetic attachment to trust.
They have a plausible credo supporting their progress,
expressed as a shrewd aspiring self-righteousness.

We should allude to the simultaneous coupling,
and merging the reasoning powers of,
the Heisenberg Uncertainly Principle,
Causation Theory applied to Historiography,
and Set Theory using Boolean Algebra.

Disparate variables compel a new set.
There is meaning to too near and/or too far.
Either of strict selected facts or participation,
give meaning to good historical narrative.
Causation questioning verifies a scrupulous assurance.

We are really only what the Cassini Space Craft
photographed from Saturn one determinant day.
Self-neuroprotection is a lasting endeavor
a textual concept that sees the world,
truthful in form, as is, delusion exempt.

Evil

Evil exists in the minds of Men.
For those effected it sheds and drips
a permanent acid stain on their paths.

The traces of having been present,
is a slowing down of rationality,
disguised in an act of punishment,
with leverage to deceive their intent,
even from themselves in performance.

As evil is peeled and revealed,
in the discourse of stripping
its existence to the core,
men and women fall injured,
their empathy colors the ground
red with blood, their psyche preyed on,
an essence trampled underneath.

And then, there is evil exposed,
caught looking at itself in a mirror,
in all its misshapen identity,
witnessed with such personal pain,
inflicting a torture of the heart.

It is a curse to realize and appreciate evil,
reminding us it is only in the minds of Men.
It is a sin perhaps, unable to act from righteousness,
or fear of St. Michael's deliverance.

It was a horror once to realize when evil appeared,
as an apparent phantom of shapes reflecting good,
revealing a kind of favorable unpolished angel,
the bearer of light seeking my approbation.

Good Men still fall to the wayside.
They may be described as casualties.
Solutions evade most wits as to its cause.
Trying not to accede to evil is difficult.

If you do will it make a difference?
Moving on after an infliction is all most
are prepared to do for themselves;
others may be more obtuse or wretched.

And therein lies the heart's pain.
For the while though, evil inflicts the soul.

The Political Event

If I chance upon you who may know
my mind and heart would you
be prepared to say so?

Sometimes speaking is the answer,
as difficult as that may be.
The eyes sometimes say more.

If I chance upon you who may not
want to know my mind and heart,
would you be prepared to speak to that?
You may not want to know.

Sometimes speaking is not the answer,
as easy as that may be.
The eyes give much away.

Knowing that I am secure in my mind and heart,
and want to know your mind and heart,
would you find that easy to speak about?
Or would it be difficult?
The eyes express compassion.

If I chance to know your mind and heart,
and you chance to know my mind and heart,
this is where speaking is the most difficult.
The chance is often witnessed as vulnerable.

Often things just go unsaid quickly thereafter,
realized from the moment of anxiety,
often repeated with skill and alacrity.
The eyes quickly demure.

The mountain becomes too high to climb,
the water becomes too swift to swim,
and the opportunity for human contact,
drifts further away diminishing to a quietude.

The Governors Choice

Vying for an appointment by a Governor,
on any level to serve a citizen duty,
is like climbing a rock face without protection,
and having a bee sting you in the neck.

The realization of holding on or free falling,
is beyond your control, only the result matters.
If one has not paid their dues early on,
the matter generally rests where one is splayed.

Socrates never paid dues to speak with power.
By his hand the self-imposed slow death
was the final gesture of his free will;
what no man was as free to take but him.

Socrates continual questioning upset many.
They had to think to consider the events.
Somehow when no money was offered,
suspicion and envy evolved the powers of defeat.

His life in the agora was a free will in virtue,
to ask questions of those in unison of thought.
His agony at death was to not allow any man,
except his own hand to control the events.

My pocket was always empty of change.
My virtue, honesty, experience, and knowledge,
was the currency I offered to the powers.
The agony of never being chosen is a protracted pain.

The agony trouble is a process inflicted by and of the State.
The scales of Justice often relent to the politics of ignorance.
Virtue is replaced with indifference and defeated with
pelf barriers that must be overcome by the supplicant.
Logos is buried and least possible ever to be resurrected.

"Crito, I owe a cock to Asclepius;
will you remember to pay the debt?
The debt shall be paid," said Crito;
is there anything else?
There was no answer to this question; ..." *

The death of the conversation,
virtue, honesty, experience, and knowledge,
brings silence to bear; the eventual
agony of the agora by silencing the Socratic.

How long should this last?

* *Ancient Greek Philosophers,* Jowett Translation - Phaedo

Alone

We are born alone.
We die alone.
We are placed deep in the ground alone.
Or, we are placed in an urn alone.
Sometimes we are spread over the earth.

Alone with the earth we will be,
mixed with the eternal material,
eventually cast into a black hole,
stripped of our light,
except our particle energy.

So, what is it about living life,
that we think is not alone?
We commence into eternity alone,
wishing, while we are alive,
we could travel with another.

Thoughts or delusions are first to conceive,
before we express, we think alone.
Our brain then acts alone to initiate.
So why is it we think
we are not always alone?

We only contract with others
to relieve Chronos,
deceiving ourselves we have
a temporary place, safe from
the hostility of the temporal
and material in conflict.

It slows our concept of
entering into the continuum of space,
where there is no suffering,
our energy expended exploding,
into the universe at death.

The disposition of the Soul
serves the course of fate,
The present temporality,
by virtue, is how we navigate.

The past is past.
The future has not yet happened.
The present is only real.
How we steer fate at the moment,
determines the future effect on Chronos.

The process determines where on
the continuum we are,
between time and space,
place and death.

Afterlife

At this point in life my pedigree and papers
have been set aside; dead are all the anointers.

It wasn't so much the aging process,
as was the pressures, duress and stress.

Throughout my career a line was never crossed;
the strict observance of dos and ethos, never chaos.

I among others, now sitting at home are not of much good,
say the clear-thinking credential committee brotherhood.

The "gray hairs" is what they called us,
because we could perform well, fearless.

The reasoning was we had seen everything,
at least we did well without much erring.

So, don't think too much about your own career,
or you might be admiring yourself as a souvenir.

Step aside gracefully at a point but not too early,
recalling you were regarded, before they wrote your elegy.

An Idea in Stone

A block of stone we turn into a statue
is generally one man's idea of an image,
manifested in a shape larger than life,
perhaps a metaphor for having once lived.

Statutes are a temporary conveyance.
They allude to life or death in a place,
representing a history as it evolved,
at times a troubled voicing breath pierced by time.

When they fall from grace in historical affairs,
we judge rewriting history, redirecting the future.
Some have stood for as long as mythology,
or as long as forgetting a poem that conceals.

The measure of civilizations images,
personify and intensify who we have become,
or seek to support propaganda formed,
once ideas are shaped into a cold stone.

The vagaries of the Bronze and Hellenic periods,
their stone chiseled by composing hands,
preceded by Egyptian Sphinx antecedents,
descended into the perfection of Roman art.

Often this transfiguring mythology changed gods.
Expressed in modern times there has been
as many remnants of the silent voices of history past,
interpreted, but never a meaningful present lesson.

One should suspect the robust forms,
or images we acclaim to understand
as the fallen remnants of the State;
replicas of what you should think.

Sometimes appropriate, sometimes not,
the forms are in custody of what we have learned.

Jesus or Shi

One Hundred Years
For Jim

Some Men step forward right into the day.
Some Men step backward into retreat.
Some Men step to the side from harm's way.
They all have in common some direction.

Some of the Men are never reticent,
but they are all the subject and object of,
"If I can make you believe I am weak,
then I can control what you think."

Some Men pace forth, walking straight into life.
Some Men take years to learn an explication.
Often some Men are inclined to silence,
advancing their measure with kind resignation.

They set their sturdy course under an open sky.
Though at times they are queried to believe
and observe a sail billow with no wind.
Their placid silence leads not to analysis.

Contrary, the Shi craft pilots toward the sextants star.
The engines are of unknown origin,
whose bent is to appear forceless.
Therein lies the schemes strength.

When Men step forth to meet Shi,
they can opportune to reconcile the variance of,
deception, fluidity, illusions, if recognition
is authentic, unvarnished and forth coming.

Whether you are of Jesus of the Occidental,
or of Shi of the deep Oriental,
how you live your life, shall reflect the light,
that emanates from the deepest part of your mind.

Shi is there to be discovered without a mask,
for those to see again, for those who never saw,
for those who learned through the years of regret,
the superlative inimical worst of human wit.

The Contours of Fate

As one arrives in a place at the heart of any substance,
there arises the stress to continue transcendence,
to not get stuck at any one level for long.
The realization of the form one takes outward,
has been a recurrent circadian cycle of awakening
at dawn to consider the mix of a day of fate encounters.

Inescapable is the desire to join with another's soul.
Desirous may be another's politeness to cross boundaries.
Even for a moment these desires are the fate skirmishes,
that lead us to who we are and the becoming of
our apparent orderliness defining our metaphysics.

To Slow Time

Passing through a threshold,
there anon appears a door,
a dimensionless shift of perception,
to reach a new place of center.

Once the angst of facing the threshold,
is diminished when occasioned,
passing through the door can be,
heartening to anyone's Primal Journey.

In Memory of Betty

Betty Thompson MD
1934 - 2019

At times there are events in life that set a direction.
We look up at the many stars lighting the way,
and we begin to see one shine by definition,
with such clarity we are compelled to stay.

The light envelopes us embracing its meaning.
It draws us near to begin the humble descent,
of learning a discernment and skill acceding,
in the deep cerebral cavern of consent.

Mentor and student weave a splendid course.
There appears no doubt why words are few.
A spirit rises and the ego passes perforce,
on a high moral plain veiled in virtue.

The tenor of sentiment refined and fashioned,
as time slowed the journey of professionalism,
the two standstill images part and reawaken.
With empathy she conferred the scepter of altruism.

In the end before the time of passing,
we long still, to look up to the stars with desire.
We see the light clear now when praying,
with a sense of happiness, virtue, that does transpire.

Her merit was a partnership with John.
Like the famed parable of the Oak and the Cypress,
they were intertwined but separate at each dawn,
standing firm but leaning in joined together, timeless.

Her roots were in the firmament of time,
Kathleen and Scott, in her shared hours.
She kept pace to a ceremonial paradigm,
a formal salvation of her life with prayers.

The Final Roll Call

Donald D Trunkey MD
1937 - 2019

With a glass of wine in hand and good fellowship
what Don casually revealed was empathy in conversation,
as might be suspected from the following voice.

There are many things I do not know.
There are many things I do know.
Somewhere in between I am still
enjoying the adventure of learning,
though death will deprive me
of this experience soon enough.

For the moment though my heart
pulsates with silent poetry,
guiding the drift of my red blood.

After I turn my last page,
the curious who remember,
may pass by and recall the ghost places,
where the seeds of learning were planted,
and empathy was offered restrained and genial,
during times of unsourced discourse;
the friendship was of splendid respect.
For all, time does declare its silence.

These were most likely moments,
of life's extreme clarity and full potential;
the whisper of Don's presence,
and a replete legacy left to the child,
from deep within a complicated man.

Who we have loved in life,
the devotions, the special sentiments of birthright,
what we have learned, grasped,
and taught, the promises we held dear,
for those whom we have mentored,
is the legacy we manifest,
at our moment of stillness.

To Read the Masters

To read a poem and invite it inside my brain and heart,
to learn about the mysteries the words impart,
to let it stir my soul inclined to surrender to the unknown,
is to live my life everyday vulnerable to the cotyledon sown.

To perceive the Masters' voice my ears cannot bend to hear,
to allow them into my imagination's chimera without fear,
to perceive them speaking to me with their power of influence,
is to grow and realize my potential was never about license.

To connect their language with what they wrote in volume,
to read and dwell in what they narrate, and presume,
to understand how they unconcealed themselves to share,
is to drink pure water and breathe deep clear air.

A lifetime is sometimes what it takes to endure,
the process of surrender to their spirits allure.

Part II Thoughts About War

The Coffee Bean Essay

As a boy growing up, I did not know the reasons for wars being fought. During my education in college and subsequent years of graduate and postgraduate work there seemed to be a cloud of anti-war sentiment that loomed over our country. It became clear to me that reproduction, sequestering or trying to share resources, culture and religion were four primary reasons for historical and recent wars. Combinations of reasons and subsets of parts always participated in the excuses for battle. The disciplined inquiry into things as an adult was the best way to identify the parts of who we are and how to think about how we find ourselves in predicaments of war. Ignoring the potential for war should also be considered.

I started this inquiry visualizing a coffee bean resting in the center of a table. It must be shared between two people, who are sitting in chairs at opposite ends of the table. They have to consume the bean in equal measure between them or else one will starve to death if the other eats more of their share. Both have teeth so they can accurately incise pieces of equal portion submerging extra temptation.

Each observes the other with a strict eye satisfying the primitive insecurities of a frail trust. Every alternate minute bite of consumption allows survival.

When the last bite is ingested by the opposite person who tasted first, then both survive well. Individually having eaten just enough, allows the other to go free from the event of dividing a resource. There was never enough for others, only for the two in question.

This dilemma is a hard act to accomplish between two people. Suffice it to say it is easier to control people, convincing them you and they are of the body. We know there are places where people who are about to be fed together squander some resources to do so with comfort. The others must starve. Stalin and Mao were good at this prescription. They knew our nature well and few would object to the result magnified.

With the best of intentions, and as the arbiter of success in the end, acquiring resources, reproduction, culture or religion has never been effective without war or stress leading to war. From the coffee bean to the land mass, our nature speaks in all of us. It matters not what one person or side wants; two must consent, or sometimes three.

The above narrative does not come from God or the gods. It comes from our level of consciousness, perhaps a phylogenetic mistake occurring in the soup that other species do not share who have limited awareness of self. They do not fool themselves with a delusion they can control any outcome of reproduction or events about sequestered resources. It comes from our neurobiology and us alone!

The Manifest Nature of War

I

The real nature of the world is a mystery,
from the inner iron core to the outer silicon surface.
Heat from accretion, formation, friction, and radioactive decay,[1]
is a thermal history of conduction and convection in flux.
We occupy some level of transience in appearance,
apposed next to a life-size stone mirror imaging ourselves,
as a symbol short lived in any manner of timekeeping;
such a small spectacle to have mixed with the sphere.

There is no voice in the layered black Vishnu Schist,[2]
a dark polished layer of silent granite,
a metamorphosis chronicled in the bottom layers,
long before our existence related to any river valley,
pressed and uplifted to be warmed by the sun's rays,
visibly a mystery to contemporary events.
Nothing seemed to happen in that 2 billion year
deposition stratum under pressure turning into a foundation.

It would not predicate we were to species dominate.
Certain things had to happen with methane chemistry,
sea water composition and several massive cosmic asteroids.
An extraterrestrial event of random gravitational attraction,
most recent, occurred to allow our ancestors to walk across
the plains of a land mass not to different from today.
We were upright, with an opposing thumb and some curious
weapons scheming for food, prey, survival and cunning.

We were the indiscriminate sediment chemical precursors,
when the stone was being formed to eventually manifest itself.
The trilobites disappeared eons before our initial chemical
complexity prepared the long sleep of origin and evolution.
Our beginnings were slow but directed by environment.
The dawn deifying our myths evolved so long after.
We threaten ourselves just looking into our future,
standing next to the inert stone monument we require.

This and any other stone we may endure next to,
can be a metaphor of us as a darkness imperfect in life,
a staid image of difficulty coming into the light of conflict,
an identifiable moment in a dim light of emerging hope,
or a metaphor of us where time and death is a moment,
both inseparable from the moment of occurrence.
As silence may have permeated over our beginning,
we still can't imagine ourselves having existed primitively.

A stone can be a trope, a hardened opposition,
that exists inured as time completes any geologic agency.
In its mirror today we chronicle the war god's hubris.
It can be a symbol of our resolve to be conditioned
against aggression or our commitment to allocate resources.
The stone then becomes a permanent exemplar,
fixed in its insistent position indifferent to life;
one example of the conflict of man vs nature.

Managing ourselves is the problematic part.
Individual managing survival and comfort needs
is an inward inflection quite opposite a stone's
anthropomorphic life we assign to it.
It is an inert symbol in a complicated world.
This can be best explained as an encasement or obtuse
declaration or palliation of those moments in life,
to never have to follow an order to cause destruction.

The politics of a state is irreverent to history.
The underpinnings of war are uniform in history.[3]
Our identities, culture, needs, hegemon ambitions,
deplete our potential to survive into the future.
The reasonings for this can be scored in an array.
Adding nuclear devastation and an HEMP[4] to the rank,
may change things to reflect and surpass the past violence
of a meteor collision or the imagined formation of our moon.

We at times encourage ourselves to turn to the stone,
spartan, laid bare, burnt, rotting done, bones laid out.
But all we want to do is go home and be left alone.
The advantage we have is to avoid someone else's war,
and everyone loses which-ever way it goes.
This world is replete with truth-Sayers and nay-Sayers.
Both are of a kind who seek resources to aid their comfort,
lives, and family propagation but who don't have an inner self.

Some are against war as a conviction of their truth,
almost or actually sensed as a deep visceral ache.
Others may find themselves in the midst of the out of control,
the juvenile anger who personify themselves leaders
of the multitude, attitudes explicit of the worst of us.
Come to think of it we have never been without war.
The crack in the foundation we either fix or repair.
The troubadour of any war ancient or modern is us.

We stop voicing the mental melody right before
the greed of battle when we hear our Generals call.
They call to capitulate your life for their life to continue.
You become blind surrendering, succumbing to animus.
The problem since Homer is the chain of command.
Agamemnon had to feed from his men's resources.
If an association becomes a conflict of sorts as we seek
to combine a resource, what is our material essence?

We are political in nature as conflicts emerge.
Really, our essence comes in a small box
about the size we can look into while appearing
to comfortably engage oneself with arms folded,
satisfied, comfortable, complacent, in need.
We try to equate culture with a number of political natures.
Our need of justice and humanitarian efforts do though,
allow us to examine hubris as a mix to the balance.

We are in need to rediscover Cicero's injustices.[5]
We must stop alloying the psychological trauma of death,
instead help the destroyed lives of wars aftermath.
Our sum, substance and core keys are simple.
It is the number of people we control.
They help us gather our resources to provide.
The simplicity in the idiom of our self-expression,
is buried deep in the stone mirror of reflection.

If we choose, and it is a choice
to not have power over others,
we come home to our childhood,
innocently sharing some meager succor,
to normalize the opportunity of being.
As we practice this humility over time,
disguised as a necessity of life,
it can strike unrest in those who must acquire,

comfort needs, reproductive safety,
or those with a genetic predilection to rule;
their needs are to discharge you into the invisible ether.
To them you become not of the body,
not of the shared spirit or are otherwise
sought out when you express empathy.
You will be placed in some peripheral margin,
unable to acquire any power or control over yourself.

II

The stuff that make wars is passionately inspired,
ingrained with profound conflicts of interest.
Money and greed are a threat to the supply of resources.
Simple control of others not in conflict,
is the root of suffering and the death of war.
We cannot convince the solders otherwise
during their course, but only in the beginning.
They must be separated individually.

Trust in their message is not to be considered.
Stop them in their tracks and take off their boots.
For those believing in the fervent substance,
teach them the dilemma of the conflict early,
but do not teach them how to use the sword.
Blood ends in the darkness of quietus,
born from inflicted cuts, penetration, or ruptured skin.
Make no mistake some will pick up the sword anyway.

In spite of the nature of the conflict,
they will lead others in defense of themselves.
The best outcome will be for us who know
how to balance fire and ice in unison.
The conflict between rule of law and justice,
will always be present with those who never speak up,
or are overcome with enmity indiscriminate in their nature.
Either way both will be consumed with war,

and the self-conflicts that lead up to nation ruin.
As for the leaders who respond in the juvenile,
with nuclear weapons at their disposal and intention,
they know not their threat to use them may turn real,
real enough to never experience an advanced behavior,
beyond their suspicions and apprehensions uncertain.
It seems there are three psychologies at work in life.
Launch a missile because one can when provoked.

Don't launch a missile because one will realize the
destruction may be complete, irreversible and a coda.
Employing the Warring Strategies[6] to the same conclusion.
We still maneuver the Occidental and Oriental domains.
We play hegemon allocating resources not yet in conflict,
or conflict not yet in dispute of supplies arising from,
individual friction and political blood flowing,
seen as red with distrust, roughness and quarrel.

We were left with hope as Eliot,[7] Seferis,[8] Mandelstam,[9]
Brodsky[10] and Joseph Campbell[11] closed their chapters.
One was raised indeterminate from $E=mc^2$.
Above the atoll's flat surface reflecting the strange,
blinding awesome Light and Cloud of power,
we were witness to our successes.
The antecedent irrefutable slow deaths were reminiscent,
and manifest in the histories of Stalin and Mao.

One hundred million estimated by their Marxist rules.[12]
Intimations of cultural shock by extinction,
all in the name of re-education,
diminished their resources needed.
The world was awakening trying to offer hope.
Our awareness today sees only a conclusion;
fusion with a perverse Malthusian curve;
an inspiring expectation of chance and probability.

I went from the Lone Ranger to Jesus' life as a parable,
as an outlier in denunciation of the Nicene Creed,
trying to discern a possible right and wrong power,
an absolute resolute proficiency outside any cultural norms.
This was against what the psychologist say is impossible,
trying to judge the right and wrong of a higher order,
touching for a moment the bliss of its mystery,
where we can actually reach beyond cultural boundaries.

We should be beyond gravity acting on our conscience,
that may bear on us to metamorphose in a chary retreat;
thinking about Hawking's belief of 100 years left.[13]
We have nowhere else to go but see the wonder,
of our imagination as it ponders having opened
the secrets of gravitational waves in another galaxy.
Outside of culture we can judge right and wrong.
This has nothing to do with being a world citizen.

It has to do with seeing beyond who we are,
and the minute conflicts we so prize, winning,
in the marketplace of sequestering resources.
Quite like if fusion were harnessed and applied,
why would we have any conflict of staying warm,
being fed, nurtured in the mind's activities without fear.
It seems so simple to listen to the coo of the doves.
We tell our truth and people drop to the side.

We are a threat to their reality who won't play,
thus starts the conflict on such a simple basis.
It expands into the irrational quickly with prejudice.
Many soon believe in the mantra and friction of envy.
We have but a specified time on this indifferent Earth,
witnessing our image reflected by other's behaviors,
and by our own hand and mind we see ourselves
only able to make war or factions, not a lasting peace.

Changing into something else while sharing
a coffee bean is an obligation contrary to hope.
Hope takes into account the possibility of success.
Being manifest is a factor of a hundred years left.
A blind ignorance of homo sapiens, even thinking ones,
who stare into the sun and expect to see in its light,
should convince everyone we must be beyond culture.
It is the only sovereign remedy from the effects of the True Believer.[14]

Notes from The Manifest Nature of War

1. K-40, Ur-238, U-235, and Th-232 radioactive decay are the heat generator elements that keep this earth warm inside so molten iron circulation may influence the physics of the internal earth composition. A very complex environment.
2. The Vishnu Schist is about 1.8 billion years old. This layer of granite rock is visible in some areas of the Grand Canyon and in some of the quieter float areas. It draws one inward respecting a silence, imagining something that old, as you reach out to touch the layers with your hand.
3. "The Manifest Nature of War" poem reflects the causes of war. They are, Culture, Reproduction Availability and Fitness, Religion, Allocation or Consfication of Resources. No single cause is always sufficient. A combination of sorts is quite plausible to escalate a conflict.
4. A HEMP is an acronym for High-Altitude Electro Magnetic Pulse from a missile nuclear fission explosion in space, that can deliver an electrical energy pulse over a large area striking the earth. The resultant electrical dysfunction will vary depending on the energy released. The effect will make inoperable many, if not all, electrical instrumentation in the affected area of high energy dispersal.
5. Cicero's Injustices are two: the first is in the manifest clear committing and carrying out of an injury to another, often in the pursuit of riches as the root: the second is not helping one who is being injured or fail to protect another from injury when they are able, often without probity. After Cicero: De Off, 1. Vii.
6. The history of the Warring Strategies in China should be of interest to Americans. There are modern and remarkable social-political changes occurring in China today. The concept of "shi," should be studied as a trait of Chinese thinking overlaying the competition for the world hegemon position. Read the *The Hundred-Year Marathon* by Michael Pillsbury, 2016.
7. TS Eliot's influence comes at the end of the transcendental tradition.
8. George Seferis believed in the hope of peace. His diplomatic experience was extensive. He represented Greek aspirations during his long career working toward Greek independence after WW II and the partitioning of Cypress. His hope in Cypress was that a lasting peace would occur. He won the Nobel Prize in Literature in 1963.

9. Osip Mandelstam died in a Siberian Gulag in 1938 indirectly by the hand of Stalin. His poetry was written, preserved, and memorialized by memory during and after his life. His circle of friends and colleagues preserved his legacy before and after being exiled from Moscow in the 1930's. Nadezhda Mandelstam, his wife, wrote about their exile from Moscow before his final imprisonment in a book titled *Hope Against Hope*, 1970, 1999.
10. Joseph Brodsky lived somewhere between space and time. Between these two hostilities slowing time down by the impact of poetry, (Mandelstam) verging toward the infinite and godless eternity (Brodsky), he was exiled from one empire only to live his life out in another. He won the Nobel Prize in Literature in 1987.
11. Joseph Campbell closed his life chapters with the concept that the earth is isolated and in a solitary orbit. He does not exclude life on other planets but what we have is probably all there is. The person and life of Jesus Christ is actually a parable pointing to man's potential. Following your bliss is a recommended mythology personal goal.
12. Stalin and Mao were the great mass murders of the twentieth century. They, for the most part, isolated, starved, murdered, and re-educated their populations in the central parts of their respective countries for a decade or more. By the late 1990's Communism of various types around the world was estimated to have killed an estimated one hundred million people. Read the *The Black Book of Communism*, 2000.
13. The sentiments of Stephen Hawking concerning one-hundred years left to find another planetary human habitat is best explained in his books. The causes of war are not traditional anymore. But the traditional can and will most likely lead to destruction and devastation. Survival within a civilization context will be problematic.
14. The True Believer is described in the book by Eric Hoffer *The True Believer*, 1951, 2010, and many subsequent printings.

Distant Thunder

The quiet nature of distant thunder in war,
deepens our senses and quickens fear;
our instincts protecting us from ourselves.
At a distance we wish for an abeyance,
a suspension from direct contact.

The sheet lightening looks like
cannon fire bursting over death.
A fusilier sees his last sight looking up
to the red and purple clouded sky.
The sounds of crying are a whisper.

The battle usually happens at dawn,
or perhaps at sunset where the gas
rolls slow over the fields of burnt cinders,
blackened skeletons, and pocked surfaces,
coming to inflict a quick death.

The living sustains the guilt.
The whisper disappears into silence,
somewhere seated in the encephalon,
disturbing our center, splaying our instincts.
The silence disintegrates our identity.

A Warring Strategy

The concept of the Shi
is an alignment of force.
Chi is the vital energy within,
from which movement and
breath draw strength.

If I convince you I am weak,
I can control what you think.
But even though I am not weak,
you will respond with indifference.
and fail to grasp Shi.

That is your weakness,
in spite of your Chi.

The Turn of Nuclear Events

The True Believer President,
preceding the right circumstances,
will manage the antecedent descending events,
usually by chronic submission, recurring
surprises, passivity, and capitulation.

The juvenile absolute despot in common
with a delusional paranoia presentation
and puerile brain development,
will throw the switch causing a cavalcade of
descending destructive consequences.

Can it be otherwise?

A Bad Dream

We all have thoughts that drag us down.
None of us are purified in life's experiences.
Periodic bad dreams are a consequent
component of a bad night's sleep.
We are engineered to accept the blind results,
as a coarse memory in the manner of morning anxiety.

Weighing in on this unconscious density,
is a wrestling of past accreted anxieties.
It is manifested as a stiffened chest wall,
labored breathing and a feeling like the
diaphragm is stuck pushing upward against
a muscle tone long forgotten in youth.

The self-punishment we endure concerns,
the injustices of a dreams unconscious effect,
looking backward on our inflicted youth,
and all the adult mistaken judgements,
about us finding our way in life.
It is severe enough to cause a woeful awake day.

But not as bad as a friend volunteering for duty,
shot three times and ending up in a marine body bag.
Perhaps prior he thought the bad dreams would go away.
They didn't and with the many, similar mistakes happened.
They lie deep in dirt under gravestones and cremated parents,
forever beneath the spreading roots of the Elm trees.

Those left alive may have been stopped early,
to have taken off their boots marking a moment
of judgement perhaps for themselves by chance,
before any bullet found its mark to silence the darkness.
They seemed to have paused long enough at night,
to awaken and forged an answer to the strife of dreams.

The Culture of War

Culture is so common it despises rationality,
wrapping the mind up in a cloud of differences.
The musing distinctions are used by Men,
as in any felicitous historical frame of reference,
against anyone who refuses to believe differences
can be put aside to live in peace without war.

In any given period of Time there are Ideas by
chance and prominence which last with irony.
They are unique and sometimes repeated.
The differences are accentuated blind,
becoming important only because,
they strike deep into the psyche of possibility.

Art as an Idea arises from culture and looks upon itself,
eventually shedding prominent culture parts,
as judged in the mind's eye sooner or later.
Some culture Ideas have an aura so impulsive in nature,
they blend virtuous soil with the hands of anyone,
who has sowed the potential for grace and splendor.

As the Ideas ascend diverse gradients they expose
the wrongs and scions which terminate deep in flesh.
For some the option next is to destroy the notion,
institution, skin color, cultural attachments,
disembowel one's identity and throw the fragments
to the animals of flesh consumption.

War becomes the operation of restoring the
weeping sores and eventually repeating the propaganda.
The cleansing effect takes two generations
to wash the psyche while preserving the atrocities
as some kind of history seen in books or poetry,
written long after the healing effect of the flesh.

Finding a Mate

The blush of a high school glance,
may favor one in emotional competition.
The longing look and the first kiss,
should cause a scent intensity and attraction.

It is the process of finding a mate,
sublime in the beginning events,
at times draws a friend's jealousy,
and many responsive discontents.

From adolescence to adulthood,
the rendezvous are skillfully assembled,
until the experience bursts with confidence,
and the mythology of passage is revealed.

Those who have hindered proclivities,
compete at the same level of desire,
nurturing their notions and self-image,
they try by imitation to acquire.

It is all about numbers and availability,
those species propagation propensities,
that we mix in with love and devotion,
that lead to behavior and specified chemistries.

The availability of reproduction liaisons,
the psychologists tell us has dependent conditions,
on the reality concerning rival successes,
or conflict begins with those of disaffections.

How do we endeavor from when we are first favored,
to accepting the spoils of war, the normalcy of knave
institutions and embracing so many who are discontent?
A nation calls on young men to risk the grave.

A Religious Belief

We are a species who must believe in something,
or so we are told by the priests in faithful dress.
Some special belief systems raise critical questions.
The answers are inherent in the questions;
no special need to disbelieve in any outcome.

The confluence of a belief or position of intransigence
delivered and a system with corridors of intra-analysis
of thought until your will is broken down,
and you become the product of a structure fulfilling
all the biological needs of a hierarchy,
is syncretism or pure flotsam propaganda.

The sermons are delivered on high, so high,
no one can argue for or against in the usual fashion
of a belief that directs an enlightenment.
It is argued "my god" is the only god and there
shall be no other as a placeholder in faith and belief.
Perhaps or perhaps not.

We are a species by chance that exists;
a very narrow set of circumstances.
If we are to survive our planet must evolve,
in a balance until it encounters the red giant sphere.
As a species we must become our potential,
or wrestle with a massive extinction singularity,
and contravene any agency in a world we might have had.

We are inclined for our survival,
as the exact opposite of how we are disposed.
War is always on the horizon somewhere.
The tension is so simple, so why fight any war,
over the explicit taut anxiety of god's?

It all started with an ancient pantheon.
The effect of one god evolved in a settled order,
sublime in the allocation of allegiance,
in an exposed métier with symbols and gifts.
There were combinations with other deities merging,
a god's mercy conferring a special status blessing,
as if there was a disposition to conceive and link.

Our evolved problem is the Earth and Science.
Unified, they are together an inconvenience,
hurtling in complete blackness tethered by matter
and anti-matter to no circular end only to
repeat its motion within a void so vast,
space may curve in on itself as an iteration,
that is part of a bigger spinning galaxy.

A possibility at an event horizon,
is to go through the black hole unscathed.
Wouldn't that be something to try?
The idea of war would be diminished to a point.
Questions of science would prevail,
over questions of mythology and differences.
Are we sure that is what we want?

The black hole cares nothing for differences;
either naked nuclei or travel to the other end intact.
Who knows, but religion plays no part.
War will always hold us back from discovery,
and pin us to a belief system where differences shine,
never to find shores in common uniting a rivers flow;
the divine in the human and the human of the divine.

If we can't muster control of our impulses,
the event horizons cornering our future options,
stone to sand, idea to dust, time to infinity,
curiosity to stillness, will cease to be interactive.
We will be deprived of the laws of physics, chemistry
and biology which act in common with all of
space-time which we perceive and can glimpse into.
The internecine conduct still rules us though, you and me.

We need a remarkable but essential paradigm shift,
so that metaphysics and science can claim their rightful place,
illuminating the actual unknowns in cosmology,
versus the structures of hypotheses.

It is essential to stop the purely secular march into the unknown,
as an eventual black hole repository into which everything
turns to nothing that we can see, or have a belief in.
But a black hole is a collapsed neutron star,
whose matter can recycle throughout the universe again.
Any belief in the divine has always been about the unknown.

Perhaps we are really a chance self-benediction,
within ourselves and an exiguous unique
phenomenon only to meet our species demise.
The last of us may witness the Earth's progress
into a future inside the goldilocks zone of providence,
propagated to an end by war and religious avidity.

Perhaps the Unified Field Theory when realized,
will unite our metaphysics and scientific hypotheses?
Perhaps war then will never be fought over such
secular science without moral judgements,
or a confused metaphysics mutating into parables,
instead with a humility that can help improve our souls;
that intangible part of us so defined we do have
under our power to refine its goodness and potential.

Conflict Within

The requirements for us to be the same is low.
The requirements for being an individual,
is almost beyond reach to those who desire.
The pressures to conform can keep you up at night.
The individuality one might express in thought or conduct,
draws envy straight from those with bloodless hearts.
They feed on your energy and consume everything good.

You are never allowed to compose your Yin and Yang.
You are never allowed to center your Chi.
You are never allowed to see the invisible whole,
the whole that is greater than the parts.
You are never allowed to see masculine and feminine,
or any historical context from a display of causality.
If you do you will be suspected of some betrayal,
by the long-standing game players who seek
satisfaction in your failures and the manipulation
plans they lay out for you to trip on and fall.

The cause of conflict falls within the self.
The self of the personal search for power,
often disguised as an endeavor of conciliation,
blaming another for no fault of their own.
The fault lies within those whose heart
is cold, left untended, taught, indoctrinated.
Their inner sight is defective without empathy.
When you tell someone the truth it is denied.
Concealment of the soul is dishonest.

The war within themselves seeks a way out
to fight the war aspired to, and the continued war within
cannot accept defeat because of the hearts' darkness.
To not be spiritual is sometimes as bad as being spiritual.
The loose ends are those that can be discarded easily.
Those in charge are like Icarus when they shine,
they deliquesce into the ether to not be seen again.

The psychological variances today are well understood,
expressed by a lexicon buried in the deep brain;
the mental outflow and inward censorship
of those who desire and profit from the work of many.
They are curious but shallow without acuity or substance.
They seek to tell their stories with a smile,
leaving their stratum messes on the table of discussion,
minimizing any semblance of a righteous life.

The remnants of conflicts are always destructive,
if not at the moment, lasting into the light,
airing inequities, posing as shadows,
or engendering offenses, reaching an apogee,
you sometimes just have no individual power to stop.

Competition for Resources

The consciousness of War ought to mirror what the mouse discerns,
as bait for the alligator who dispatches and consumes its prey.
Something has to happen to one which to the other is adverse.
The appetite is insatiable day after day, hour after hour,
never to quit, only a small reprieve by the clock for a rest,
merely to gather again to exhaust and consume a quarry.

We are so much alike in our need of constituent requisites.
A competitor for nourishment to feed our discrete cells,
the individual component parts that make up our whole,
the whole developed from a process of convergent evolution.
We are malevolent to ourselves and our kindred are enemy prey.
The process is not abated with an efficient population reduction.

That was tried by Robespierre, Stalin and Mao.
Precious metals, rare earth metals, oil, are what we feed on,
in conjunction with evolving a possible Class 5 planet. *
We have begun to fathom our biosphere as contiguous.
We have evolved beyond the expectations of hermeneutics,
only to witness ourselves as beyond the essentials of a wood fire.

It is expected that nuclear fusion would solve our problems.
It would facilitate us and permit a wood fire to keep us warm.
Considering reducing consumption to a population of one-seventh
of today can only reflect on what we are and have become.
We are the arbiter of the evolved planet Earth and ourselves.
We can do one or the other, but probably not both, probably not.

Probably not presupposes!

The Light of the Stars: Alien Worlds and the Fate of the Earth by Adam Frank.
2018, Page 219. * "Class 5 planets have agency-dominated biospheres."

The Dinner Table

The days used to be long in my youth,
as a measure of a kid's time,
leaving our house after breakfast,
with a quarter and a dime,
not having to return for lunch,
if we wanted to spend our pocket money,
playing at the park or swimming,
skin bare in the cold pool briskly.

Returning for dinner was the
only option if we wanted to eat,
and 5 o'clock was the time to arrive,
clean hands, washed face and neat.
Silence was the order of the meal,
watching the news across the room,
hearing about the battlefield casualties,
of the raising Vietnam gloom.

Douglas Edwards and Walter Cronkite
were the voices in succession.
They peaked my father's interest,
at the table with habituation,
cutting his steak and potatoes,
with a knifes precision into pieces,
small enough to consume the news,
without the mastication noises.

Since his 1941 draft status he did not
serve in WW II or Korea's menace.
The railroad was all he understood,
and that was his record of service.
He was remote from war and all its casualties,
horrors, odors and sepsis.
He just wanted us to know something
was wrong with the world so venomous.

That was the start of my realization,
seeing the images of a soldier's helmet,
chin straps hanging down beside
their ears so the shock of a bullet,
did not rip their head off when struck,
wearing uniforms that didn't fit,
sleeves rolled up because of the heat
and humidity without any benefit.

When I look back these images
are what I remember firm in mind.
As life evolved into adolescence,
all my images became intertwined.
I lost all innocence with the
Twenty-One Gun Salute as it ripped
my ears and head in two, since then,
still hearing noises from the crypt.

I played in the shade of the birch trees
and climbed their branches,
to sit out my youth high above
the curb being careful to not take chances.
I only came down when my mother
called me for dinner at 5 o'clock.
Then time would change from a kid's time
to another time of TV and war talk.

Another Origin of Conflict

It all starts out innocent enough, that is, boy meets girl.
It never ends up though in happiness valued like a pearl,
lasting in love, sensitive commitment and passion,
with the same person apposite in achieved absolution.

Someone else always gets in between the girl and boy,
widening the experience of one of them in a game of coy.
This is the normal search pattern for the mating competition;
the widening experiment determines chum complexion.

So, one falls into traps off and on seizing the moments of allure,
being attracted to secondary best and sometimes to the paramour,
the local flavor of what is safe and emotionally a detached neutral,
only to get confined in the downward spiral of the oppositional.

The sexes are unequal for various reasons of biology and condition,
trying to mate in an attractive pattern of behavior and permission.
Widening the notions to include culture, religion, and scarce resources,
the female chooses from experience tempered with trespasses.

Or, at least sooner or later and it wasn't always that way.
The burden of war was losing and missing your next birthday,
or enslaving women and children for successful insemination,
and the winner's propagation into a state of future facilitation.

War as an Outgrowth of Culture

Right and Wrong are values steeped in culture prior to a judgement.
When the Right or Wrong fails is when the culture fails.
At times the outcome of a decision process is failure of an arrangement,
pertaining to a Right or Wrong weighing on blind justice scales.

The hunt for power often goes against the sentiments of the Agora.
Dissention and discussion divide the tribal impulse to support a position,
the Right weighing as part of the tipped blind scales cause uproar,
the kind that leads to self-destruction, disintegration, and partition.

War is a not so perfect solution to solve a predicament.
It does decide the imperfect winners and losers who moralize,
and think it plausible they may win the cultural amalgam argument.
Those who are Wrong will yield a price that ushers their demise.

To understand war as an outgrowth of culture and how it evolves,
deep digging is required to read how parts of the human brain interact.
The worst illusions are born from parts which seek to absolve
the motives, passions and intellect of an unanticipated cataract.

Memories of Growing Up

No one ever knows why love
dissolves between two people.
Sometimes the wind shifts,
a cold weather front moves in unnoticed,
the temperature drops and one says,
it seems to be colder now.
The children hold one parent
in contempt for some time,
never letting anyone know,
they are striking out to be loved.
The other parent is an attachment,
a security not letting go,
where apparently love may
occasionally reside with a secure hug.

The children know there is
no safety net cast to help.
They now have to begin,
to figure out things on their own.
The anxieties begin at night,
when they are under the covers.
At least until morning,
things are not as bad as they think.
Going to school at the start
of the day is most uncertain,
when they are asked to accomplish
the obligations of learning.
Their compass spins slowly,
unable to resolve any certain bearing.

Occasions in the Fall when anxiety
begins or prevails can be grievous,
similar to adults who experience rejection
in September and pain in October.
One day the leaves are green,
then the cold sets in soon enough.
The leaves turn red, brown, and yellow,
seasoning the Fall fallow colors.
Perhaps one day later they begin
to rustle in the wind, drop and spin
downward in a telescopic fancy,
leaving bare stick branch tracings,
in the night silhouetted under,
the luminous late harvest moon.

The feeling never really leaves,
as time passes or depression resumes.
Clearly subdued but incessantly never
entirely gone from the psyche,
surfacing in dreams as a tough
tug of war with the subconscious,
in those light sleep patterns,
three hours before dawn's awakening.
The deep seeded memory of streets
with windblown leaves before the rains,
can raise an intense inward feeling,
of alienation in hearts open to be loved,
intensifying any step forward,
that would relieve the pain of existing.

So, what course do we advance with awareness,
nurtured in our hearts that never goes away?
Being maligned perceptively or really,
is frequently a combination pairing,
always leading to a sickness
within the heart not easily overcome in life.
As children orphaned from the parental love,
of a narcissist in gray clothes,
continuously wanting to be loved,
or raised by a parent who suffered abuse,
love can slowly dissolve compelling
extensive differences in attempts to love.
To be on one's own and reveal,
a safe self-image in the mirror is difficult.

In time the memories may go away,
but return at moments unexpectedly.
In time the memories are only
able to be restrained with virtue.
In time the dreams tend to get
more difficult to confront or vanquish.
In time having paid one's debt to Asclepius,
may be the only peace of heart.

The Making of a Disturbed Person

A child cannot stop crying,
fear has changed their nurtured trust.
They hide in safe places,
like the monkey who is about to strike,
like the baboon who is about to kill,
or the gorilla confronting the invaders.
They have three side protection,
with an escape route just in case,
crouching in a low profile to gain refuge,
from their pain of living.

The adolescent scurries about aimlessly,
seeking affection at times resting
too long under the apparent care
of a loving hand, only to quickly
move away to avoid feeling vulnerable,
while admonition is inflicted.
They experience the push and pull,
asking for love only to be refused,
deepening the schisms forming,
in their small immature brains.

Or, experience the invitation to be loved,
by those who will reject them,
a frequent power behavior,
of the adult narcissist who has been scarred.
Children quietly endure a gnawing starvation,
with troubled distended bellies,
when painful love is pursued,
rejected and normal is on the wane.
The cerebral paired lobes wither,
and the integrated fissure waxes.

We know these things to be true
as a child grows up becoming.
In spite of the phylogenetic propensity
to violence in our makeup,
we do little but stand on the sidelines,
witnessing the abuse,
clinging to the idea of the parental right,
to abuse skirting the law,
by interpreting parent abuse behavior,
as within proprietary rights.

We should be careful how the child
is raised and cared for.
The making of the disturbed,
in a demented fashion appears to be easy.
There are no golden sunsets,
when the conflict is internal and constant.
It makes for a worsening life,
when personal and sexual identities,
are developed from pain, deep seeded anger,
rejection and sham love.

The Making of a Disturbed Soldier

The making of a disturbed soldier is easy.
First you have to dehumanize each in a group.
All the partial identities must line up to be counted,
the digit numbers are assigned left and right,
tight so the nexus does not break rank.

Answer to one leader who has certainty,
and you don't have to think about yourself;
all are one suffering alliance together.
The persuasion is propaganda excellence.
To engender a thought raises a barrier for all,
except the one leader who trammels liberty.

The needs are food, water, sleep, warmth,
rifle, knife, blanket, compass, and clothes.
Those who don't believe have trouble
putting on their boots and lacing them up.
They give no thought to the simple oneness;
messengers not of a divinity but of death.

The orders are easy to follow, just conform.
Add in the basics of Making a Disturbed Person,
and The Making of a Disturbed Soldier is complete.

For us it becomes easier to sit on the sidelines observing.
Later it also becomes easier for us to dehumanize our brain,
as we often become complacent of what the result can be.
By doing nothing the outcomes are predictable.
The soldier's weapon does not have to be fired just loaded.
The disturbed soldier's identity does not have to be discrete,
just tight within the nexus but at the outer limits of the senseless.

War is in the Heart of Man

Our world tends to chaos,
it matters not what happens
day to day in our adventurous bliss,
fate will lead us,
or, whether Entropy actually increases
with an approximate cost.
We at some point realize we cannot resist
the ordered universal set.

If we don't believe there is a god,
then we are unsure of the idea.
If we do believe in a god,
then we are sure of the existence,
by saying it is God's plan,
from the book of Isaiah.
Pascal did go to church to hedge
his bet though, just in case.

Irrationality is part of the order of any day,
preceding and during our short time.
The irrationality is about the noble sublime.
Wordsworth's verse of losing innocence,
as a child growing up can be praised.
His tenor of thought in time reveals war;
a part or circumspect between his lines;
the sublime of the dispossessed.

Culture sure can make an argument,
heated when transgressed upon.
Even within a culture thought adjustments,
evolving can splinter a heart,
with well-meaning glances, atonements,
recognitions, and ethos.
Living life often is laminated,
like a geologic fault exposed with many layers.

The randomness of dopamine receptor activity
even if channeled, is a biologic function,
restrained sometimes, or expressed as an affect,
nuanced as conversation eventually causing disagreements.
Therein lies aggression, maneuvering
suggestions of being greater than one.

I keep looking for the basis of war,
only to find myself looking into a mirror.
Some days I don't like the reflection,
some days I don't like the mirror.
A reflection does tell me
when I have not listened, or witnessed,
the causes of love turning into rejection,
or friendship dissolving.

The Manifest Nature of War is beyond
the individual heart offerings.
The Marxist Historian looks at Causation
as a proletariat set of facts and circumstances.
But War does start with the individual,
hubris, a predisposition,
narcissism, and a fanatical belief
to be able to alter history to cause fate.

To transform the coming future
into reality from the present pain,
suffering may cease.
There will be better light to find the way.
The pain and fear of existence
will be an illusion and sleep will be peaceful.
The transformation will be remarkable
after propaganda successes.

I was not at the Battle of Omdurman
or at the Battle of Poltava.
I was not at the Battle of Antietam
or at the Battle of Vienna.
I was not at the Battle of Ia Drang
or the Tet Offensive, or part of Iraqi Freedom.
But like a soldier I was prepared,
for violence by my football athletic coaches.

To crush the opposition on the field
creating a fracas wound,
was of course permissible,
as long as it didn't show after the game.
I believed in the mantra of the coaches,
as helpful to becoming an adult.
It was psychologically an elixir,
to keep one growing up right.

Time helps the evaporative process,
halting the propaganda.
I was headed to the drain hole,
where the water essential for life
drains so you become a plug,
definitely at the murky bottom.
Resistance to sinking or free falling
in this large repository is futile,

You have learned violence and soon after
would be the time to climb out,
head above the horizon to see,
why everyone else didn't succumb,
to the same belief you did that might,
made right on and off the field.
This was the way and manner
to grow up behaving as a leader.

It would be so easy to fit into a Marine Unit
after signing a contract.
The identity of all who eventually fall,
is paid with blood sacrifice,
having their youth taken away;
some with 3 bullets in the heart still beating.
It's a tough way to learn the virtues
of the enemy in that split second.

The enemy that survives may very well
not be a stellar person.
Mind sets of religious fanatics,
tribal beliefs, land is for the collective,
or the mechanisms greased,
for the continuation conduct of war,
is sure to entangle all reasonings,
in the hubris of hegemony.

The seven deadly sins, Dante's nine circles of hell,
modern psychopathology, all comprise
historical attempts to describe our evil intentions.
Hubris, narcissism, will to power,
fear, sex trade, mind altering drugs,
scarce resources, social oppression,
all keep us distracted with war.

We should raise above the exigency,
to initiate ourselves from aggression,
and the two ingredients of sovereignty and morality,
these bursting forth modern cranial problems.
Yes, that is where the location is for all of us,
good or bad in nature to historically change.
It seems we have only just begun,
to focus as our biosphere is unceasing.

Our Possibility

As I lay here looking up to a very blue sky,
in a position of repose,
my life and opinions having been
well examined about to close,
I only hope the wise of the world,
will prevail and war will cease,
having been taught violence
early in life but now desire peace.

We are of a social code and anatomy,
that teaches the violence to fight wars.
The elements leave youth simply vulnerable,
to persuasion and generate deep scars,
sitting in the mind growing up,
augmenting acts of being and personality.
So much is possible with positive temperance
of teaching about love artfully.

War is our single part once eliminated,
will allow us to survive,
granting a choice to harness fusion energy,
to provide a future alive.
Our planet will move on into its future domain
with or without us.
Our choice is to find that Socratic Virtue
within out potential vastness.

ABOUT THE AUTHOR

Writing five books of poetry has been a fifteen-year history prior to and after my academic retirement. Composing musing thoughts has been a lifelong process. The evolved writing it down has developed into a journey into the self and the imaginative process to see what may come forth for others to appreciate. Life intensifies and takes on a purpose at some point in time. This purpose of growing the self and soul is slow. Somewhere between childhood and a capable adult that point in time will present itself.

The most difficult aspect of writing poetry is to expose the personal self. Telling the truth, using language that enriches the experience is important. You have to get over the embarrassment of revealing yourself to yourself, friends, others who are strangers, and to your children; to be, do, and write who you are. Eliminate distractions, vexing persons, bad habits, and focus on the inner self. It is difficult to do your best, which as it may turn out, isn't always your best. Writing from the heart is good practice. My mentor used to say when you have set the writing pen down you should ask yourself the question "What have you done for the reader?"

I hope the ideas presented in this book will provoke thought and what is possible arising out of what is.

DWA
April 2020

DOUGLAS W ANDERSON graduated from Lewis and Clark College in the fields of History, Biology and Natural Science. For 30 years he was a dentist anesthesiologist practicing at Oregon Health Science University School of Medicine Department of Anesthesiology and Peri Operative Medicine. He is retired from clinical and academic life. He lives in Sunriver, Oregon.

www.ingramcontent.com/pod-product-compliance
Lightning Source LLC
Chambersburg PA
CBHW022304060426
42446CB00007BA/589